F IN SPELLING

F IN SPELLING

Summersdale Publishers Ltd
46 West Street
Chichester
West Sussex
PO19 1RP
UK

www.summersdale.com

Printed and bound by CPI Group (UK) Ltd, Croydon, CR0 4YY

ISBN: 978-1-84953-649-3

Substantial discounts on bulk quantities of Summersdale books are available to corporations, professional associations and other organisations. For details contact Nicky Douglas by telephone: +44 (0) 1243 756902, fax: +44 (0) 1243 786300 or email: nicky@summersdale.com.

F IN SPELLING

THE FUNNIEST TEST PAPER BLUNDERS

Richard Benson

summersdale

Contents

Introduction

We've all been there: exam season is getting nearer and nearer, the multi-coloured revision timetable has come out and any semblance of a social life has completely disappeared (apart from scheduled five-minute conversations with your mum to break the monotony). But when it comes down to it, and you find yourself sitting at a rickety desk in a cavernous sports hall with a blank page before you and a pen in your hand, what happens? Nothing. The information you spent weeks drilling into your brain is gone, leaving you clutching at any remaining crumbs of knowledge in the hope of a mark or two for effort. Or worse still, you have the facts at your fingertips, but a pesky letter or two falls out of place, rendering your answer ridiculous.

But never fear! This brand-new instalment in the bestselling *F in* series is loaded with answers where creativity makes up for lack of comprehension and spelling is something you really don't need to worry about too much. You may not get your desired grade with answers about *Charlie's Angles* or environmentally friendly turtle power, but you'll have the exam marker in stitches!

Subject: **Biology**

What part of the body is affected by glandular fever?

The glandular.

Name a living organism that contains chlorophyll.

The Incredible Hulk

Biology

When an organism's genetic material spontaneously changes, what is it called? Give an example.

An X-man. When Logan grew bone claws and changed his name to Wolverine.

Name two types of fat found in food.

1. GOOD FAT
2. BAD FAT

What sometimes happens to skin when it heals after having been grazed or cut?

It gets scared

Name the five senses.

1 Nonsense
2 Suspense
3 Insense
4 Common Sense
5 Seeing Ghosts

What is the generic term for birds that hunt for food primarily via flight?

Birds that pray.

Explain the meaning of the word 'myopic'.

It's when someone makes a biopic, but about themselves.

Name the largest part of the digestive system in most vertebrates.

The bowl.

Give an example of a meal that might contain a high level of protein.

Grilled chicken beast with vegetables

Biology

What's the scientific term for a living thing?

An Orgasm

Name some of the purposes of antibiotics.

To protect against biotics.

What body part expands and contracts in order to allow the human body to control the movements of its limbs?

Mussels

In order to survive, plants must sometimes compete with other plants. Name two things that plants compete for.

Runner-bean races and jumping-bean competitions.

Biology

Explain how plants compete.

*Most plants play fair,
but Venus flytraps bite.*

Explain when monkeys and apes began to evolve, and
explain how.

*It all started when
they went through
an evolving door*

Explain why Darwin's theories were unpopular when they were first published.

He suggested humans
are descended from
apps.

What is a pathogen?

A killer gene

Why is it important to help prevent the extinction of plant species?

BECAUSE OTHERWISE WE'LL NEVER EVOLVE TRIFFIDS IN REAL LIFE.

Why are antibiotics ineffective in the treatment of flu?

My mum says flu doesn't exist— especially man flu. She says Dad makes it up to get out of doing chores.

What are the negative effects of regularly smoking cannabis?

It makes your clothes smell

You run out of money

Regularly running out of cannabis

Subject: .....Chemistry..........

Name a metal element that burns with a bright white light.

Magneto.

What is the carbon cycle?

An expensive kind of bike.

Chemistry

What makes up the structure of an atom?

Quirks.

Give two examples of hydrocarbons.

Pepsi & Coke

What do we call the chemical reaction between a fuel and an oxidant when heated?

FIRE! I love fire.

What is the process in which sugars convert to gases, acids and/or alcohol?

Puberty

Chemistry

What is a polymer?

Something you use to fill the cracks in the walls.

What is the chemical formula for water?

Tap + turn = water

What three elements need to be present to start a fire?

1. Sticks
2. A match
3. Something to light the match on

What are nanoparticles?

The tiny pieces that grannies are made of

Chemistry

Explain why diamonds are hard. What can diamonds be used for?

They're hard to stop your jewellery getting damaged. They can be used for rings, watches and tooth implants.

Why is methane a gas at 20° Celsius?

Because that's the temperature of a fart.

Who was Humphrey Davy? What did he invent?

He fell off a wall before he could invent anything.

Why is Mars red?

Because it's embarrassed about Uranus.

Chemistry

Why does bread need to prove?

It has an insecurity complex. It should really be happy as it is.

Why did Mendeleev leave gaps in his periodic table?

He just needed some time out due to PMT.

Subject: ....**Maths**................

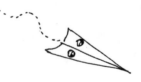

Maths

Draw a trapezium.

weee!

How do you calculate the volume of a prism?

Count all the prisoners.
The more prisoners,
the louder it will be.

What is the name of a six-sided polygon?

Sixagon

Two friends share £18 at a ratio of 6:3. How much do they each receive?

An unfair amount, if one friend is getting more than the other.

Maths

Is money 'continuous' or 'discrete'? Explain your answer.

My money is 'weekly' and 'pitiful'.

Write the number 32545346 in words.

Three two five four
five three four six

The probability that Steve oversleeps is three times the probability that he does not. Work out the probability that he does oversleep.

Depends - is it a Monday?

Draw a polygon.

Jane works in a cafe. She wants to work out if more men than women eat cake. Design an observation sheet for her.

Name three types of angle.

Charlie's Angles: Sabrina, Jill and Kelly.

Define a pentagram.

SOMETHING YOU USE TO SUMMON THE DEVIL.

Define a triangle.

The most boring instrument in the orchestra.

Subject: ......**Physics**..........................

What are fossil fuels?

What you need to power a dinosaur.

Where and how are fossil fuels extracted?

Mostly by grinding up old dinosaurs.

Physics

What are lasers used for?

The main weapon on the Millennium Falcon

How is burning fossil fuels harmful to the atmosphere?

The smoke makes you cough.

What type of electricity production harnesses the power of the sea?

Turtle power

Give ways that a homeowner can generate and store their own electricity.

Invest in a human hamster wheel.

Physics

Explain ways that a household energy bill can be reduced.

Tear it into small pieces

What determines the pitch of a sound?

How angry the person making it is.

What is the name of the effect of a sound changing pitch as its source changes position in relation to the listener?

The Duplo effect.

Why do the windows steam up on the inside of a car on a wet day?

Because it's too rainy to snog outside, so people have to do it in their cars.

Physics

How does a puddle of water disappear after a rain shower?

It ejaculates.

What does 'thinking distance' mean in terms of a vehicle stopping?

It's the distance you drive when you think of something you left at home and you have to stop and go back for it.

What affects braking distance?

It depends on when you last stopped for a brake.

What is a hybrid car?

Chitty Chitty Bang Bang.

necessary
necessary
necessary
important

Subject: ...... *English* ....

What is one of the key themes running through *The Diary of Anne Frank?*

Anne Frank's Dairy had lots of cows running through it.

Name a book written by Jerome K. Jerome.

Three Men in a Boa.

Miguel Cervantes was writing at the same time as Shakespeare. Can you name his most notable work?

Donkey Hote.

What is the technique called when a writer uses the weather to reflect how characters are feeling?

Pathetic falafel

Lord of the Flies is often described as 'terrifying'. Describe an incident in the book which is terrifying.

The bit where all the flies come out at once is quite scary, but it's hardly The Evil Dead.

Many believe that Piggy suffers the most in *Lord of the Flies*. Do you agree? Give reasons.

Yes, it's because they make him into an escape goat, because he's named after a farm animal.

What do you think of the way Elizabeth behaves in *Pride and Prejudice* on meeting Mr Darcy for the first time?

She acts very a loaf.

What are your first impressions of Mr Darcy?

He has very good manors.

Write about the character that has the greatest effect on Scrooge in *A Christmas Carol*.

The Ghost of Christmas Present, because he reminds Scrooge to buy Christmas presents.

Write about the importance of animals in *Of Mice and Men*.

The mice are very important – without them you'd only have the men.

English

Explain the meaning of the word 'dystopia'.

I had dystopia once
after eating a bad
burger.

Explain what a colon is. Demonstrate how it should be applied in a sentence.

It's a kind of perfume for men.
You spray it on your neck to make
yourself smell nice.

A competition has been launched to find young people to join an expedition to the South Pole. Write a brief letter to persuade the organisers that you would be a great asset to the team.

My mum says I have a warm personality, so I wouldn't get cold. I also like penguins.

Subject: Religious Studies

What event in the Gospel of Matthew contains The Lord's Prayer?

The Serpent on the Mount.

What is an icon?

Lady Gaga

Religious Studies

Explain what an orthodox church is.

A place for religious
people with bad backs

What is Advent?

The season where you
get a small piece of
chocolate every day.

What is fasting?

Not half as exciting as slowing.

What is an agnostic?

I'm not sure.

What do you understand by the following commandment: 'Thou shalt not commit adultery'?

You shouldn't pretend to be an adult if you're not one.

Is life better or worse if people observe the Ten Commandments? Explain your answer.

Anyone can observe them, but life is better if people actually do them too.

Explain one commandment and how you apply it to your life.

'Thou shalt not covet thy neighbour's ass" means it's OK to look, but try not to stare all the time, and definitely don't touch.

What do you understand by the term 'afterlife'?

It's a computer game that some people get addicted to.

Can God's existence be proven? Give an example.

I heard someone say 'Thank God it's friday' last friday.

Explain the role of a bishop.

It moves diagonally and can be used to trap the king.

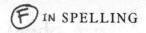

How is a rosary used?

It goes well with lamb or in Itelian food.

Explain why rings are exchanged in marriage.

To show that you have bondage.

Give examples of vows exchanged at a Christian wedding ceremony.

For butter or for worms.
Till death do us fart.
For Richard our pourer.

What is the purpose of prayer?

God knows

Give the names of two symbols found in a synagogue.

Usually, you shouldn't play the symbols in a synagogue.

What happened at the birth of Buddha?

He was born

Subject: .....**Music and Drama**.....

What piece of equipment can be used in situations where a stringed instrument can't be tuned by ear?

An electronic tuna

Who sang the soul songs 'Respect' and 'Think'?

Urethra Franklin

What musical structure is commonly found in classical music by composers such as Mozart and Beethoven?

A sympathy.

What do you understand by the terms 'homophonic' and 'polyphonic'?

One doesn't like gay people and the other doesn't like parrots

What is 'a capella'?

A small Italian hat.

To which family of instruments does the clarinet belong?

Clarinets are part of
the wind-producing family.

What is a riff?

A thing Elizabethans wore round their necks.

What is the time signature of this extract?

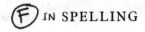

In *King Lear*, what theme is most present when Edmund says, 'The wheel is come full circle'?

Car Maintenance.

Write about the character in *Romeo and Juliet* for whom you have the most sympathy.

I have most sympathy
for the audience

What advice would you give an actor playing Romeo?

It's just a teenage crush - you'll get over it.

How does Dylan Thomas present Willy Nilly in *Under Milk Wood*?

He keeps him in his trousers.

Write about two characters who have power in Arthur Miller's *The Crucible*.

All of the witches have magical powers.

Subject: Classical Studies

Which civilisation established the first known use of democracy?

The Ancient Geeks

What is the common translation for the famous phrase 'carpe diem'?

Catch of the day.

← Mr Jones

Classical Studies

Why did the Romans steal the Sabine women?

Because they didn't know better.

If you were a publicly owned slave in Ancient Greece, what jobs would you be forced to do?

Pubicly owned slaves worked in temples and other pubic buildings.

What was a herm? What was its purpose?

It's at the bottom of
a toga, to stop the
ends from fraying.

How did the men's room (*andron*) differ from the women's room (*gynaikon*) in a Greek house?

The andron has men in it and
the gynaikon had women in it.

Classical Studies

Explain the difficulties of robbing a Greek house.

If you try to rob the house after a big party, the owners would probably hear you come in because of all the broken plates on the floor.

Who was the reputed king of the gods in Ancient Greece?

Zeus

Who or what was a Cyclops?

The sound of a horse riding a bike.

How did Medusa change from a normal woman to a creature with serpents for hair?

PMT.

Classical Studies

Who or what was Pegasus?

Pegasus are what my mum uses to hang out the washing

What monsters appear in the *Odyssey*?

~~Aliens~~

~~Giant Sharks~~

Velociraptors

Why would you require a strong voice to perform in a Greek tragedy?

Because you'd have to speak up over all the crying in the audience.

Who were the Argonauts?

They were people sent up to the Moon in the 1960s.

Classical Studies

The ancient Romans didn't have calculators. What did they use instead?

Their fingers

What didn't Roman children enjoy about education?

The same things I don't enjoy, such as exams like this one.

Describe a Roman dinner party. How is it different from a modern dinner party?

There were more
Romans there.

Who was permitted to wear a toga?

People going to parties

Classical Studies

What was Roman life like for women?

The same as it was for men, because they all wore dresses.

Name one living person who visited the underworld.

Kate Beckinsale

What is a fresco?

A type of coffee - with froth
on top.

Subject: **Media and Business Studies**

Give an example of a media product aimed at a niche audience.

The Antiques Roadshow app.

What does 'self-regulation' mean in the context of media industries?

Deciding not to watch a whole series in one go on Netflix.

Explain how a media star can promote themselves using the Internet.

Putting a naked selfie on Instagram is a good way.

Explain the importance of niche markets to media industries.

They're where media people buy statues and other knick-knacks.

Give an example of 'invasion of privacy' in the context of media industries.

Big Brother

What are the important qualities of a successful soap opera?

1. Being screened during the day.

2. A big enough student population to stay at home and watch it.

Media and Business Studies

Suggest three ways to promote a new soap opera.

1. Give away free soap.

2. Give away free opera tickets.

3. Include plenty of sex scenes.

How do television companies conduct research into their audiences?

With cameras inside TVs.

What is an ISA?

She's a cute girl in my class.

What does APR mean?

It's a short way of writing April.

What is a standing order?

" Stand up, now! "

What is the security code on a credit card?

621.

What are the vital ingredients for a successful action film?

1. Bruce Willts
2. Explosions
3. Car chases

Give a two-sentence pitch for your action film idea.

The lead actor is Bruce Willis. There are explostons and car chases.

How can live streaming of reality shows cause legal problems for its producers?

If somebody dies during the show it suddenly turns into dead streaming, which is horrible for everyone.

Jane has raised money for a fun day at her school by selling cupcakes at lunchtimes. Give three other ways that she could raise money.

1. Put the money in stacks
2. Put it on shelves
3. Hold it up high

The fun day requires a risk assessment before it can go ahead. What is a risk assessment?

Too risky to say.

It's the day of the fun day. What are the ways that Jane can assess whether it has been a success?

Ask people if they had fun, and count the bodies.

What does 'fair trade' mean?

When you swap your best comic for a really rare action figure.

How does 'fair trade' benefit others?

It stops people getting beaten up in the playground.

Name one important piece of equipment needed to set up a wireless network.

A rooster

Subject: .....P.E..

(Physical Education)

GOAL!

In athletics, name three types of jumping event.

High jump
Long jump
Tripe jump

What sports category do skateboarding, scootering and surfing fall into?

Bored sports.

P.E. (Physical Education)

What must you do after exercising to prevent muscle damage?

Worm down.

Give examples of 'anaerobic activity'.

Zumba is an aerobic activity. So is Boxercise

What effects can excess weight have on the body?

Heaviness.
It makes you fat.

Give reasons why exercise helps a person lose weight.

They are so busy
exercising they
have no time to
eat cake.

P.E. (Physical Education)

What is a person's metabolic rate?

I would have thought only robots have metal bolics.

What is the Fartlek training method?

It consists of farts and Daleks.

What two qualities are important in order to be an effective sports coach?

Wheels and comfortable seats.

Explain two ways in which an amateur sportsperson can secure funding.

1. Theft.

2. Bribery.

P.E. (Physical Education)

Give three examples of active leisure activities.

PlayStation, Xbox, Wii

Subject: **P.H.S.E**

(Personal Health and Social Education)

P.H.S.E (Personal Health and Social Education)

What umbrella term is used for the police, fire and emergency services?

Pubic services

Explain the benefits of being outdoors.

You can fart and people might not notice

What information should you have on a CV?

Mostly lies, but only if you're sure they won't be found out.

What is a domain name?

The Iron Islands, The Wall and King's Landing are all domain names.

P.H.S.E (Personal Health and Social Education)

What is phishing?

A hobby where you catch
phish and sometimes crabs.

Bob's computer has a virus. Explain what a computer virus is.

Something your
computer catches if
you sneeze on the
keyboard.

What is anti-viral software?

Medicine for computers that are prone to getting viruses.

Give one potential health problem that could occur as a result of people using ICT equipment for long periods of time.

You are more suspectible of getting mindgrains.

How would you prepare for a job interview?

1. Cover up my 'I hate work' tattoo.

2. Stop drinking at least half an hour before the interview.

Subject: ...... **History** ......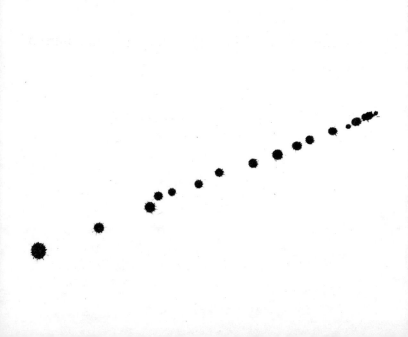

What is the Revolution of 1668 also sometimes known as?

The Goriest Revolution.

Name one reason why the Pyramids are still admired to this day.

They are feet of engineering

What happened to those who opposed the Nazi regime in World War Two?

They were often sent to constipation camps.

Who is the longest-reigning monarch in British history?

Queen Victoria, she sat on a thorn for 63 years.

Who were the Bolsheviks?

A Russian ballet company.

Who was the last tsar of Russia?

Tsar Nicholas the Last.

Explain the reasons for the Wall Street Crash of 1929.

Too many cars on the road, and bad drivers.

Who was Malcolm X?

The great - great - great - great - great - great - great grandson of Malcolm 1.

Describe how Hitler took over Austria in 1938.

Quite quickly.

Explain the reason for the erection of the Berlin Wall.

To hold up the Berlin Ceiling

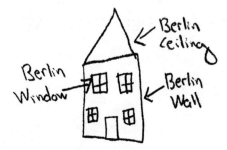

Who was Yuri Gagarin?

THAT GUY WHO BENDS SPOONS.

Explain the dangers of life as a cowboy in the American Midwest.

High risk of being shot by Clint Eastwood.

Who were the Mountain Men, and why were they important?

Characters in
Game of Thrones
— very violent.

How was the Black Death dealt with?

By dying, usually.

What were the Swing Riots in the nineteenth century?

People were angry about
Rubbish playground equipment.

What was the New Poor Law?

The opposite of the old
Rich Laws.

What is the theory of the four humours, and how did it influence the prevention of diseases?

If you laugh four times every day you won't get sick.

Describe public health in the nineteenth century.

A bit like public health in the twentieth century, just older

Subject: Geography

Geography

What theory states that the earth's continents move over time?

Incontinental drift.

How are deserts formed?

My favourite way is to combine ice cream, sliced bananas, caramel sauce and lots of squirty cream.

What is the name of Germany's fourth-largest city?

Colon.

What sort of clothing would you associate with Scottish national dress?

Scottish people like to wear twee jackets and quilts.

Name one waste product that becomes a hazard if disposed of in water environments.

Rappers

What are the Nazca Lines?

Nazca is a really popular sport in America. Lines are drawn on the road to show drivers where to go.

What causes can there be for environmental change?

When coins drop out of people's pockets while they're walking in the countryside.

What are the characteristics of a shield volcano?

It's the one that protects all the other volcanoes

Geography

How do you know when a tsunami is about to occur?

The weather presenter tells you.

How may a quarry be used for tourism purposes?

It's a great day out for tourists who like rocks.

Describe the effects of perceived climate change.

The main one is that people perceive that the climate is changing.

Give three examples of extreme weather.

1. Weather for bungee jumping.
2. Weather for skydiving.
3. Weather for tombstoning.

Geography

Explain how heavy snow can cause disruption to daily life.

People get distracted from their work by snowball fights

How do reservoirs and dams create a reliable water supply?

They write reminder notes for each other to make sure the water supply is always reliable.

Name three of the earth's layers.

1. Sky

2. Grass

3. Soil

What do we call the currents in the earth's magma?

I don't know, but I always spit them out. I hate currents.

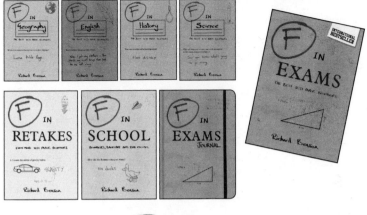

F IN SERIES

Richard Benson

The Exams are over, the results are in and just when you thought it was safe to go back in the classroom...

BANG! It's time for the F in... Series!
Enjoy a heady dose of hilarious answers that canny students have given to the trickiest exam questions.

F in Exams £5.99 (ISBN: 978 1 84024 700 8) • F in Retakes £5.99 (ISBN: 978 1 84953 313 3)
F in School £5.99 (ISBN: 978 1 84953 506 9) • F in Exams Journal £7.99 (ISBN: 978 1 84953 650 9)

F in English £3.99 (ISBN: 978 1 84953 324 9) • F in Geography £3.99 (ISBN: 978 1 84953 325 6)
F in History £3.99 (ISBN: 978 1 84953 326 3) • F in Science £3.99 (ISBN: 978 1 84953 323 2)

If you're interested in finding out more about our
books, find us on Facebook at
Summersdale Publishers
and follow us on Twitter at
@Summersdale.

www.summersdale.com